TIPS ON SURVIVING CORPORATE HELL

Randy Zinn

SOR Press
GAITHERSBURG, MARYLAND

Copyright © 2020 by Randy Zinn.

All rights reserved. No part of this publication may be reproduced or transmitted in any form or by any means; electronic or mechanical, including photography, recording, or any information storage and retrieval system, without permission in writing from the author.

Randy Zinn/SOR Press
Gaithersburg, Maryland
www.randy-zinn.com

Tips on Surviving Corporate Hell / Randy Zinn. -- 1st ed.
ISBN 978-1-953643-03-2 (paperback)

Contents

Introduction 7
    About Me 7
    Disclaimers 8
The Basics 11
    Employment Types 11
    Finding Jobs 15
    Technical Interviews 17
    Benefits 19
    Salaries 21
    Clothing 23
    Security Clearances 25
On the Job 29
    Coworkers! 29
    Communication 31
    Events 33
    The Work Day 35
    Food at Work 37
    Our Work Environment 39
    Personal Time 41
    Deadly Sins 42
It Ends 45
    Threats to Your Job 45
    Looking for New Work 47
    Impending Departures 49
    Before Leaving 51
    On the Way Out 53

After Leaving 55
About the Author 59
Randy Zinn Books 61

ACKNOWLEDGEMENTS

Edited by Kathy Macfarlane

Cover design by Randy Zinn

Introduction

We tend to think that the corporate world is a place of professionalism, where respectable adults like our parents may be working. And so when enter into it, we may be quite surprised at some of what goes on. While there are many skilled, dedicated workers, there are also plenty of slackers, incompetent peers, and bad managers. We might think these people won't be our problem, but they often are. Knowing how to spot and handle them is key to surviving, even thriving, in the sometimes murky world of business etiquette. This book is designed to help you find a greater share of heaven than hell in the unpredictable world of Corporate Business.

The tips in this book come from *The Corporate Hell Survival Guide*. This guide will provide even more extensive detail on everything you need to know to successfully navigate your corporate career

About Me

I began my career as a software developer in the late 1990s, knowing little to nothing about the corporate world in which I would spend the next twenty years. In that time span, I have been a direct employee, a contractor, and a self-employed consultant. I have created software and the corresponding documentation for my employers/clients or *their* clients. These are sometimes local governments, commercial clients, or non-profits, but they are usually federal government agencies like NASA, the State Department, the White House, the Army, Navy, Marines, IRS, and more. I have also been a software development manager.

I have also earned Microsoft certifications in my field, but my degree is a Bachelors of Music in classical guitar, Magna cum Laude, from Catholic University in D.C.; I was originally a music composition major. I've overcome many issues and know how to survive, even thrive, in tough situations. Since it is always wise to learn from someone else's mistakes before making them yourself, I hope this book will help you do just that.

Disclaimers

Many books about corporate etiquette are aimed at those who run the companies, but the intended audience for these tips is non-managers – those to whom no one officially reports. Much of the content applies to managers as well, since they also must survive the corporate world, but the advice is not about management issues per se. It is about how individuals can minimize personal and performance-related problems that can arise within their workplace. It's also designed for those who have never had a corporate job, have just started, or are early in their careers. Those graduating high school or college, intending on entering the corporate world in their near future, may benefit the most.

Your profession, employer, industry, and locale may impact how well the advice applies to your situation. Some of the examples provided are U.S.-specific. However, the corporate culture in which I work, and from which the examples are drawn, is fairly typical no matter where you are around the globe. Life may be different where you are, but most workplace issues are universal.

CHAPTER ONE

The Basics

The first section touches on everything from finding jobs, to job types and benefit issues.?

Employment Types

Tip #1: "Employment 101"

Being a permanent, salaried employee comes with various benefits, like health, dental, vision, insurance, retirement plans, and vacation pay. But there are downsides, too, like unpaid overtime, slower salary growth, and being taken for granted, among others. Learn the pitfalls so you can judge whether this is the best option for you. It's the easiest to arrange but that may come with a price.

Tip #2: "Contracting 101"

Independent contracting (a.k.a. 1099) in the U.S. is called sole-trading in some countries. We are paid by the hour and may work directly for a client or through an agency. This offers the freedom to leave a bad job (or client) with little fuss, and choose projects, commutes, and more that we want to do (instead of our company making these choices for us). But it offers no benefits and is a more precarious lifestyle.

Tip #3: "Consulting 101"

Lying somewhere between employment and contracting, consulting through our own company means we have a reliable employer (ourselves!). But that does not mean we always have clients. We can arrange our own benefits, just like a contractor, and we seem more serious than one, but there is more overhead and some companies won't do a corp-to-corp arrangement with us at all.

Tip #4: "Employees Have More Financial Security"

Neither contractors nor consultants get unemployment benefits when not working. They do not get severance, either, or matching 401k contributions that can really add up. They also do not get paid until 30-60 days after submitting an invoice, depending on the client, and this can make life difficult until we are established. Employees get paid every two weeks or twice a month.

Tip #5: "Government Contracting is Risky"

Government contracts are usually heavily contested, and always come with expiration dates. This means they can lose the contract and let us go. Or they will woo us for one contract, then put us on another that is terrible for us but good for them. We won't have much if any say in the matter, as we are expected to "take one for the team." That job we loved can suddenly become the job we hate.

Tip #6: "Employees Are Soft Targets"

If we are an employee, companies can feel more entitled to expect us do whatever they say, within reason and the law, and we can't object. This means assigning us to awful projects, giving us a long commute to offsite locations, or generally making us job no good. We have given our right to make these decisions to the employer once we come onboard.

Tip #7: "Non-Employees Are Disposable"

There's no such thing as job security, but contractors and consultants are seen as more disposable than permanent staff. They're the first ones to be shown the door if any downsizing happens. They're great fall guys to blame problems on. "It wasn't our employee, but this outsider!" There's little to no loyalty in the corporate world, especially for non-employees.

Tip #8: "Beware the Illusion"

There's an old joke that the difference between employment and contracting or consulting is the illusion of job security. The former supposedly has it while the latter don't. Well, employment doesn't have it either. It just seems like it. We can lose our job for seemingly endless reasons that can have absolutely nothing to do with our performance.

Tip #9: "Beware the Bait and Switch"

Sometimes we're told during an interview what we will be doing but, when we arrive for our first day (or shortly thereafter), we are told we'll be doing something quite different. The excuses can vary and I can't claim it's never done on purpose. But it doesn't matter. We have a new job, one which we may have quit our last job for, but now we don't want it. This is typically only done to employees, not contractors or consultants, who can "walk" more easily.

Tip #10: "A Body in a Seat is Headed for the Street"

If we are working at our employer's client, they may earn their fee for each hour we are there, whether we have anything to do or not. This is known as the "body in a seat" situation. This can seem relaxing with so little work to do, but the moment there's contract trouble, our name comes up first for someone to blame, scapegoat, and send to the unemployment line. So if we find ourselves in this position, we should try to get out of it before someone does it for us.

Bonus: "Consultants Can Lie"

If we are unemployed, we typically need to admit it on a resume, job application, or to a recruiter/hiring manager. But if we own our consulting company, we are technically employed. We may not have a client, so we're looking for work, but we don't have to admit it. They can't make us. Our client list and contracts, etc., are confidential and none of their business. This means we don't have to admit to having no income or "job" right now. We technically *do* have a job, so it's not even lying.

Finding Jobs

Tip #11: "Job Fairs Can Be a Waste of Time"

Depending on the industry, job fairs can be a waste a time. The reason companies do this is to be in the public eye and to collect resumes for their database for later recruiting efforts. Sure, they may have an actual fit for us right now, but it is uncommon. The reason for us to attend is not to hand over a resume, though we should (this can be done online, typically). It is for rapid-fire, in-person presentation of who we are and what we offer. It is practice for interviews, basically. We may get offered some on-the-spot, and we should take them. Always bring an empty goody bag to fill up with pens, mugs, and other gadgets that they're giving away, while trying not to seem like this is the only reason we are there.

Tip #12: "Use Job Boards"

The great thing about job boards is that the recruiters come to us. They are the ones trying to get our attention, not the other way around. The secret to job boards is to update our resume every Sunday so that we appear, by Monday morning when recruiters begin their week, to be actively looking. We likely appear near the top of search results. No actual change to the resume is needed. Make a trivial change like adding an extra space after a paragraph, hit save, and make sure the "last updated" date says today.

Tip #13: "Responses Are Not Guaranteed"

In life, regardless of who is initiating contact, a response is not guaranteed. Some will argue that as a candidate, we should respond to everyone, but this can be unrealistic in a hot job market when many recruiters contact us every day for *weeks*. Besides, recruiters often don't respond to us, even when they initiated contact and we followed their response requirements to the letter. There is no double-standard here. Either we're all required to respond, or none of us are. It is the latter. They'll be back later with another job whether we ever responded before or not.

Tip #14: "Avoid the Phone at First"

Avoid getting on the phone with any recruiter until knowing details about the job and whether it's a possibility worth considering. Many will call about jobs in the wrong field, wrong state (planet?), and other misfires that make it a waste of time. Oddly, they often refuse to get off the phone even after being told this and that another obligation demands our immediate attention. It is not uncommon to spend thirty minutes talking to someone who doesn't have an appropriate job right now. One reason they give is networking (see the next tip).

Tip #15: "Networking is Overrated"

Seemingly everyone glowingly talks about the power of networking to find our next job. This may depend on the industry, but it is generally overrated. The reality is that by being on job boards, our resume will slowly work its way into countless recruiting databases, held by hundreds of firms. When they have a position that even remotely fits our skills or location (and often when it's a total miss!), they will contact us. It's their job. They cast a wide net. So if you hate networking, don't force yourself. They'll come to us anyway (if our resume is good). The odds of someone we know personally having an appropriate job for us at the exact moment that we are actually looking are not great. It's mathematically unlikely. And we won't get told about the job just because we talked to them before; they will tell u. anyway! Many agencies may contact us about the same position.

Technical Interviews

These tips may only apply to programmers and others who must endure the so-called technical interview.

Tip #16: "Recruiters Are Often Wrong"

While recruiters want us to succeed and get the job, they can be very wrong about what a technical interview entails. This isn't necessarily their fault, as the company they're trying to place us at might not have been accurate. They can say it's very technical, not at all, or in between. The test can be an oral, written, or computer-based. Every single detail they tell us can be completely off. Be prepared for anything. And then tell the recruiter afterward what it actually entailed. They'll be grateful, even if we bombed it because of what they told us.

Tip #17: "Expect Unfairness"

Technical exams are often unfair. They can expect us to know things that we haven't needed to do in years (if ever), without warning. Sometimes they ask questions that don't even relate to the job. In the real world, we can look up something we don't know, but sometimes we can't in these tests. We can be expected to write code by hand, as if we do that on the job. In many cases, the testing environment does not mirror the real world. We can be unfairly expected to achieve things without the tools we would have on the job.

Tip #18: "Cheat If You Have To"

Due to the previous tip, if we have to cheat to dodge the unfairness, I consider it fair game. Two wrongs can indeed make a right. Cheating usually takes the form of looking up answers on our smartphone if we are left alone to take the test. Given the inability to prepare for these tests, it's only fair. Just don't get caught.

Tip #19: "Memorize Definitions"

Many tests consist of being asked to recite definitions of technical terms, as if this is something we spend time doing while employed. It pays to have recently re-memorized many common terms for exactly this reason. Keep an ongoing and organized list of them on a computer or phone and commit it to memory when job hunting. A snappy answer works wonders compared to a disjointed one, delivered without confidence as we search your memory for a term we haven't seen in months or years.

Tip #20: "You Can Refuse a Test"

We do not have to take a test. Of course, refusing means we do not get the job. Most tests are oral and not too bad, but the handwritten or computer tests are rough. We can politely decline the position because, in my experience, fewer than 10% of jobs require it and we can find one that does not. It is not worth the aggravation.

Benefits

Tip #21: "Benefits Sometimes Aren't"

A benefit is called that because it's supposed to benefit us, but sometimes these can vanish. In the U.S., the one most likely to do this is the matching retirement contributions the employer makes for us. We must be an employee long enough for them to start doing it, for one, but then we must be "vested." That means if we leave, we keep none of their matching, or 20%, then 40% and so on, each year letting us keep more of it. This varies by the company.

Tip #22: "Vacation May Vanish, Too"

We typically earn vacation hours for each pay period we are employed, but it pays to ask what happens when we leave the company without having used it. Do they pay it out? If so, in the U.S., they will typically decide how much cash each hour is worth and pay us for the accrued balance. If it's worth $50 and we have 4 hours, we get $200. This can add up to a significant windfall after termination. Or it can add up to nothing.

Tip #23: "Vacation Can Add Up"

In the U.S., the longer we are employed by the same company, the more hours of vacation we typically accrue, but this isn't true in some countries, where it is the same regardless of tenure. In America, it can be significant and a true loss if we switch jobs. However, employers are often willing to "play ball" and give us more than the usual offering if we ask. For example, maybe two weeks is standard, but we tell them we have three at the current job and so they bump it up a week. This is more likely if we are older as they understand we have probably become accustomed to it.

Tip #24: "Can You Go Negative?"

Sometimes we have a vacation planned. And then we are changing jobs and won't have enough vacation accrued at the new job by the time the trip starts. Always ask if you can go negative on your balance. Employers often understand plans have changed and will allow this, on a case-by-case basis, usually with the caveat that they're unlikely to make a habit of it, nor should we. It also depends on how negative we intend to go. The circumstances will determine their willingness.

Tip #25: "Keep a List of Your Choices"

We are often shown a dizzying array of benefit choices, particularly for health and dental. Once we've made our choices, write them down in detail. This helps when we have to re-do these choices the next year or when changing jobs and we need to compare how good an offered benefit package is, or simply to choose something comparable.

Salaries

Tip #26: "Avoid Admitting What You Make"

It is not a potential employer's business what we are making now or what we have made previously. What matters is whether or not we are seeking an appropriate amount for our skillset, experience, and the current market conditions. Leave that part of a job application blank. If asked for previous salary info, respond with what you are seeking as if you didn't hear the question accurately. Most will take the hint. Few will persist.

Tip #27: "Frequent Job Changes Can Benefit Us"

One of the best ways to quickly raise our salary is changing jobs often, such as every 6-24 months. The reason is that companies sometimes give no annual raise at all or the standard 3-5%. When we change jobs, we can ask for quite a bit more, sometimes a lot more, and get it, especially if we have picked up skills or certifications. And not told them what we are making now.

Tip #28: "Frequent Job Changes Can Cost You"

If we're a job hopper, this can cost us. In the U.S., the biggest problem is retirement accounts. Many companies won't let us start contributing to a 401k for 3-12 months. If they do employer matching, we won't keep any of it if we leave too soon (typically under a year), and there's often a rising scale where we keep another 20% for each year we remain employed by them. Outside the U.S., bonuses may not be paid unless we remain with the employer for a set number of months after we earned it. Leave and we are literally leaving money behind.

Tip #29: "Don't Discuss Salary with Coworkers"

Once we give out personal information, like our salary, it's no longer ours to safeguard. Even if we trust that person, they can tell someone else. We may not care who knows, but others might resent how much we make, or scorn how little. We may also learn that someone else makes far more than us despite the same skills or experience, leading to resentment.

Tip #30: "Learn Market Value from Jobs You Don't Want"

Depending on our field, we might often be approached for jobs we don't want. This is the time to ask for what amounts to a [significant?] raise without admitting it's more than we currently make. Depending on the reaction, and if done repeatedly with multiple employers, this will tell us whether we are on the high or low end (or middle) of what we could be making. If they balk at a high number, now we sense a limit, but we didn't want the job anyway, so it makes no difference if they pass on us. They won't, however; they will ask if we have flexibility.

Clothing

Tip #31: "Start Conservative"

On the first day, it's often best to dress conservatively. This means not only avoiding one extreme of casualness, but also the other extreme of formality. Showing up in a three-piece suit could be just as odd as a t-shirt and jeans, depending on our position. We just won't get in trouble for it, but looking like we take this *too* seriously isn't a great look either. It can come across as desperate, eager, or wanting to please. If we are far above what everyone else is wearing, we will need to tone it down. Keep an eye on this during an in-person, on-site interview before landing the gig.

Tip #32: "Always Reconnoiter"

Despite the official policy, we can often get away with less formal attire than has been stated. The guide here is what others are wearing, but we must know what they do for a living. Someone like a network engineer might need to get down on the floor and therefore they get away with jeans instead of slacks, but we won't. See what peers have on their torso, legs, and feet. Black jeans might pass in a "no jeans" environment. Nice mocs may pass in a no-sneaker one, depending on color.

Tip #33: "Don't Tantalize"

This one is more for women. Be aware that leaning over in a low-cut blouse offers a cleavage vantage point not appropriate at work. So does wearing a skirt and putting feet on a chair so that your knees are under your chin, the skirt falling to your hips, giving everyone a view of undergarments. Outfits that reveal a tattoo might also be a poor choice, regardless of its location. For men (usually), there's the infamous "plumber's crack" from crouching in pants that are too tight for that. Be aware that we could find ourselves in a literal position that we weren't expecting when we dressed that morning, resulting in one of these tantalizing glimpses.

Tip #34: "Keep a Layer at Work"

We never know when the AC suddenly goes into overdrive or we're forced into a meeting in a freezing room, for hours. It can sometimes be painfully cold at work and it's wise to keep a light jacket or sweater handy for such occasions. The opposite happens less often – it gets uncomfortably warm (sometimes due to AC failure) and we are tempted to drop a layer. The same solution applies – keep something light but appropriate on hand.

Tip #35: "Beware of Casual Days"

Casual Friday is still not an opportunity to wear inappropriate things to work, whether it's because of what they say on them or how revealing they are. We still need a sense of decorum. Sure, wear something comfortable. Just remember not to make other people *un*comfortable because you're wearing it!

Security Clearances

Tip #36: "Save Your Research"

When we are up for a security clearance, we will be asked to dig up all sorts of information on past residences, jobs, references, and more. Save all of this because no clearance lasts forever, and we might need to fill out the very long application again one day. Why repeat the time-consuming research into our past when we can save it?

Tip #37: "Don't Lie"

An investigator will verify everything we say on the paperwork (and at our interview), so don't lie. One of the things they're looking for is honesty, not a perfect life. If we have made a mistake, admit it. As is often the case, the cover up is what can sink us.

Tip #38: "They're Worth Money"

Depending on who we ask, a security clearance can be worth $10k-$20k a year in salary. We do not pay the cost of getting one, our employer does, and we are not beholden to them for this, though they may not like it if we leave shortly after getting it. But leaving can be an option, considering that another company might give us a lot more money to do the same job, now that we have the clearance. If you're thinking this isn't loyal, no company is loyal to their staff, so why should we be to them?

Tip #39: "Companies Need to Hold Them"

Our employer, or client if we are a consultant, needs to "hold" our clearance. This means it's been transferred to them and being kept "active." Our job requires it, basically. Sometimes we have a Top Secret clearance when the job only needs a Secret, so we must ask if they can "hold" the higher clearance. Also, when we leave, we have two years for another employer/client to "hold" our clearance or it lapses. Sometimes companies lie that they have taken it over when they didn't do the paperwork and we end up losing our clearance.

Tip #40: "We Can Get Them Back"

A clearance that goes inactive (because we aren't using it) can be reinstated with a little paperwork by our employer/client. We just need to tell a new company that it's inactive, how long ago it was last active, and they'll take care of it, if they're willing. By contrast, if our clearance has expired (they only last so long), we will need to start the process over, but it's far faster than the first time because we have already been awarded one in the past.

CHAPTER TWO

On the Job

This is the heart of our concern – the problems that come up while on the job.

Coworkers!

Tip #41: "Don't Badmouth"

No matter how tempting, avoid badmouthing people at work. And when you hear them doing it to others, pay attention: they're letting us know they'll do it to us, so it pays to not offend them. If we're keen to badmouth anyway, never be the first to criticize someone. Let someone else take the risk that not everyone in the room will agree with them or support them for doing it.

Tip #42: "Beware of Jokers"

People can sometimes jokingly criticize us, such as blaming us for something. Do not humor this, not even for trivial things, and especially not in front of other people, as they may be gearing up to do it for real later. Jokingly scapegoating us easily turns into the real thing. Generally, any negative comment at our expense is not to be viewed lightly, even if it is made lightly. It's okay to show no sense of humor about this.

Tip #43: "Schmoozing is Golden"

Conversations with peers about non-work related items get a free pass, generally, even if a talk lasts an hour! That depends on work getting done, of course, but it's considered part of bonding and team building. We're social creatures and never doing small talk with peers might reflect poorly on us. Besides, being liked can help save us from the chopping block.

Tip #44: "Beware of the Manager CC"

Sometimes we are emailing with a coworker or client, and someone CCs a manager. Tread lightly here if you're the one including them. It can be seen as tattling or putting the other person on notice that an authority figure is now involved. The graceful way to do that is to ask the manager a question in the email so it looks less like tattling. Of course, it depends on what is being discussed.

Tip #45: "You Will Be Left Out"

Cliques exist in all walks of life. We may discover one (or more) at work once hired, or it forms later, and we may get no chance to join. These can be frustrating, but remember that this is our job, not a social club, and curb the hurt feelings. Pouting has never gotten anyone invited to anything.

Communication

Tip #46: "TLDR!"

Long emails at work are not appreciated any more than long documentation is. Sometimes we are asked for the latter only to have the requestor ignore it. In fact, "too long, didn't read" is a trick we can use to inhibit a decision and slow progress. Kill the recipient with too many details or options and they'll shut down and do nothing. And if we need them to do something so we can continue, now we have some free time at work. Generally, people don't want too many details at once, and if we really must give it, do it in person. It goes down better as a conversation, not a manifesto.

Tip #47: "Beware of Tone"

Any sentiment that is even slightly negative should not be delivered in writing if this can be avoided. And if it is, we must be highly aware of tone, which can be easily read into our words. Be on high alert for your agitation levels and talk to someone in person or on the phone if negative emotions are at all present in you. Jobs have been lost over perceived tone, and lesser consequences aren't much better.

Tip #48: "Go with Defaults"

Showing personality at work can be fine depending on how it's done, but avoid changing the white background of email to something gaudy. Or using weird fonts no one can read. Or writing in pink. It is just distracting. Keep your signature short, to the point, and professional, too. No huge images, slogans, or other stuff.

Tip #49: "Read Receipts Are Evil"

When sending email from a program like Outlook, we can request a read receipt, meaning we get notified when the recipient's click on it. This comes across as "I know you read it so why didn't you respond?" Regardless of our intentions, it can be seen as passive aggressive and many people don't like it and will set Outlook to "never" give them. We can do this, too, but what's more important is to never be the person requesting them. It is overbearing. There are better ways to follow up with someone, but few worse ways.

Tip #50: "Use Your Strength"

For many of us, talking in person is superior than the phone, which is superior to email/texts. We should figure out which one works best for us and make it our default. This is especially true if we have anything negative to say. A smile or friendly voice tone can smooth over the message in a way that words on a screen simply cannot, but maybe we're the exception. Find your strength and rely on it. Find your weakness, too, and beware of it!

Bonus: "Don't Use Nicknames, Etc."

Always refer to people by name, not something like "sunshine." Some nicknames can be perceived as sarcastic, but even if done seriously, still run afoul of the annoy-o-meter. Some people are quite cynical and even cheeriness (such as "sunshine") is unwelcome. Sexist words like "baby" are also out. The best we can get away with is stuff like, "Hey man," because it's so generic.

Events

Tip #51: "Always Attend Onsite Events"

Always attend any corporate event hosted at work. Skipping it looks anti-social and casts us in a bad light. We don't have to stay for the whole thing, as we can arrive late, though leaving early is better, and it's actually better to not stay for every last second because it looks like we would rather be socializing than working!

Tip #52: "Assume You're Paying"

Sometimes we get taken to lunch during our first week. Always assume that you're paying your way because it sometimes sounds like it's on them when it's actually not. It can be hard to tell. Discreetly reach for your wallet when the check comes and let them wave you off, then say thanks. It's less awkward than the reverse.

Tip #53: "It's Not About the Coffee"

Some coworkers are fond of going to get coffee together and may invite us. Don't turn down this invite until you've accepted several times first, even if you don't drink the stuff. It's not about the coffee. It's about being social. Get a snack or water if you have to, but go. If we refuse from the start, the invites for this and other things will stop. We are rejecting them. Not wise.

Tip #54: "Humor the Birthday Events"

Adults shouldn't care about birthdays at work, but some do and celebrate them to one degree or another, like a card that's going around for signatures or even a cake and gift. We must once again participate even if we don't want to, because it looks bad if we don't. Just sign a card (we don't have to write a note), eat some cake or wave it off because we're on a diet, but put in an appearance, even if only for 30 seconds.

Tip #55: "Always Contribute to the Potluck...Somehow"

We should find a way to contribute to a potluck. Whether it's cooking, buying pre-made items, offering cash (for others to get those items), or helping to setup or pack away, this is an opportunity to show willingness to do our part, however trivial. Freeloading is a poor look.

The Work Day

Tip #56: "Be Visible"

When working from home, it's important to be visible, even if we are doing no actual work all day. Disappearing for long lunches, or not being reachable while working from home, are mistakes. The assumption is always that we are goofing around. Appearance is more important than whether we were working or not. This is why we tell others about an offsite meeting we will be attending rather than going and not saying anything.

Tip #57: "Be Transparent About Hours"

Don't make a secret of your typical work schedule. When something upsets it, be open about that, too. If you were late by ten minutes, admit it and make a point of being seen at work ten minutes past your usual departure time. We want to make a show of not skimping. Once again, appearance matters. Even if we're doing non-work related stuff on the computer for that extra ten minutes at the end of the day, it's better than not visibly making up the missed time (as long as no-one can see what we're actually doing).

Tip #58: "Assume Your Behavior is Being Noticed"

Sometimes we feel like we're getting away with something, like repeatedly being late and not making up the time, but any repeated behavior is ripe for others to remember. We will acquire a reputation and it's on us to ensure it's a good one. Even innocent behavior like doing a couple walking laps around the building is sometimes best done discreetly (i.e., *don't* be visible!). For example, randomly change where this walking is done so it's less likely the same people are *always* seeing you do it.

Tip #59: "Small Breaks Count as Work Time"

No one can work constantly without a break. Whether a few minutes or a few hours, breaks can be counted as work time if no one realizes we are not working at that moment. We are expected to be at work a set number of hours per day per week, not actually work that many hours, just close. As long as we get your work done, on time, and it's good, there is leeway for unnoticed breaks, which is the key. Subterfuge is our friend.

Tip #60: "Work First, Goof Around Later"

Speaking of not working, it's always best to get assignments done first and then goof off, not the other way around. That way, we don't have to worry and if someone gives us grief or asks to see the work, we have it at once, tossing in a "just finished!" remark (even if that was hours ago). Sometimes it pays to act like we are doing a mini-celebration, as if this is what our "goofing around" behavior was actually about.

Food at Work

Tip #61: "Avoid Smelly Foods"

Some people have a more acute sense of smell and therefore sensitivity to strong odors, which become more pronounced if we warm up a dish in the microwave. It's usually not wise to re-heat fish, and some will even object to popcorn, maybe because they now crave it and are on a diet. Forbidden food signs are sometimes posted in kitchens. If we really want to eat such items, we just don't warm them up. Make popcorn at home, put it in a ziplock bag, and avoid the nasty looks.

Tip #62: "Clean Up Your Mess"

There is an idea that something owned by everyone is owned by no one, so instead of everyone taking care of it, no one does. Don't be the one who makes a mess in the microwave or fridge, on the counter, or in the bathroom and doesn't clean it up. And yes, even crumbs fall into this category. Sometimes it even pays to be seen cleaning up someone else's mess.

Tip #63: "Eating at Your Desk is Normal"

Many places do not have a dining area, forcing us to eat at our desk. This is almost expected for lunch and certainly snacks. But this is another reason not to do smelly foods, because it isn't just people who enter the kitchen after us have warmed it up that smell it; it's everyone near us. And yes, they will know it's us, especially with repeat offenses.

Tip #64: "Avoid the Fridge"

If we can, we should avoid the refrigerator altogether by keeping food in an insulated container at our desk until lunch time, and don't leave leftovers. Bring it every day you have food from home. What's wrong with the fridge, you ask? It can be crowded, people move our stuff, name tags fall off, and of course there's the occasional theft, all of which lead to irritation with coworkers (seldom good). And we can forget it's in there and it goes bad, grossing out others (that's when we *want* the name tag to fall off).

Tip #65: "Enjoy the Free Food"

Whether it's Pizza Fridays, Bagel Mondays, or leftovers from an office party/event, free food is often put out in the kitchen or designated area, which is when we know it's first come, first serve. But don't always assume available food is for you until you know how that tends to play out at a job. It's okay to ask someone.

Bonus: "Don't Be a Pig"

Whether it's stuffing our face with something we brought or swiping every last sandwich leftover from an event, gluttony is a poor look. Going back for seconds looks better than a heaping plate. Besides, if it's an event and there's too much food, no one cares when we return for more; in fact, sometimes people are encouraging others to take some with them. But if there's too little and some get nothing, it doesn't look good for us.

Our Work Environment

Tip #66: "Less is More"

Avoid making your work area a shrine to all things personal, with every last wall or desk space covered in paraphernalia. A few choice items just looks better than every last surface covered in *something* non-work related. It is tacky, too "busy," and an eyesore. People will judge you. We're also almost certainly in the minority with this and while it's a trivial mistake, less is more.

Tip #67: "Avoid the Speakerphone at Your Desk"

No one wants to hear both sides of a work phone call that has nothing to do with them. Many consider it selfish, distracting, and counterproductive to their own needs. Hearing one side is a necessary evil, but hearing everyone on the other end, too? Do not subject coworkers to it, especially repeatedly.

Tip #68: "Cubicles Are Great"

It's tempting to criticize the cubicle because we'd all love an office, but the cube is far better than the open floor plan or a shared table. Not all cubes are created equal. Some have very short walls, are too small, or are situated outside meetings rooms or at busy intersections, where people often decide to hold impromptu meetings that we are forced to listen to. But it could be worse; instead of this being occasional, the open floor plan or shared table makes it a 40-hour week hell. Be glad for what you've got.

Tip #69: "Don't Contribute to Noise"

Being a loud talker is a genuine offense in close-knit working conditions, but there are other ways to be noisy. Playing a radio at a desk is one, as are loud calls, or even a personal computer keyboard (to replace the office-supplied one) that makes a racket. But so is the impromptu meeting right over the shoulder of your poor coworkers at their desk, when it doesn't involve them. Think of work like a library, though we don't need to whisper.

Tip #70: "Amenities!"

Some buildings have more perks than others, like in-building (or nearby) restaurants, covered and paid parking, kitchens, lounges, breast-feeding rooms, and more. Try to scope these out during interviews, asking for an office tour afterward. Even the type of cubicle (or lack thereof) or the spacing can be an issue that will slowly impact our on-the-job happiness. Don't forget a drive-by of surrounding streets and eateries to sense options for dining out.

Personal Time

Tip #71: "Make Discreet Personal Phone Calls"

Personal calls are a fact of life, but it's wise to keep them short or walk away from our desk for them. This is mostly to avoid others hearing what we say rather than stopping them from realizing what we are doing. We are assumed to be making a non-work call if seen on the phone away from our desk, but if it's short or infrequent, no one minds.

Tip #72: "Work Email is For Work"

With personal email accessible via smartphones, there are few good excuses to use a work email account for personal business. Just don't do it. Remember that they can and will read emails sent on their network. It's their right. Don't be seen extensively or frequently typing on the smartphone, though, as most will assume it isn't work related.

Tip #73: "Beware Stingy Bosses"

Some managers really frown upon our need to sometimes have a doctor appointment or other personal commitment during work hours, even if we're a parent. They may insist on us using vacation time for it rather than making it up on another day. This disrespect for work-life balance may be present in other ways, too, such as allowing us to work from home while being subtly disapproving of us for doing so. There's little to do about these stingy managers except take the hint and play along. Most are more accommodating.

Tip #74: "Plan Work-From-Home Days"

If we want to do personal things while working from home (instead of working!), the smart approach is to work our butt off the day before, don't show anyone all that we accomplished, and then pretend we did some of it while at home the next day. This way, if e are suddenly asked to produce work, we already have it. The attempt at catching us doing nothing fails. We may even feel justified in relaxing a bit at home after the flurry of activity the day before.

Tip #75: "Utilize Off-Site Meetings"

Being away from the office, especially if we are in our car, offers the chance to run an errand or two and pretend we were at a meeting longer than we were, or got stuck in traffic on the way back. Just don't go overboard with it. An extra 20-30 minutes is quite different from several missing hours. As with anything, repeatedly doing it in short succession is more likely to be noticed, so use judiciously and not consistently.

Deadly Sins

Tip #76: "Don't Take Credit for Another's Work"

It happens. Sometimes it's on purpose, and other times, maybe someone assumes we're the praiseworthy person behind something and gives us kudos we don't want to decline, so we don't. The person who actually earned the praise is likely to find out about it. Some have the guts to speak up, and this is where it gets ugly. Even if they say nothing to us, they have work friends, too, and may let the truth be known. Others also might just know. This stunt seldom works out well.

Tip #77: "Don't Step on Toes"

Offering to help someone with their work can be fine as long as we don't seem like it's because we think they're incompetent. The bigger sin is actually doing someone else's work for them unasked. Even worse is deleting someone else's work and redoing it, then handing it back to them. But aren't we supposed to collaborate, you ask? Yes, but agreeing up front that one is doing the work and the other person is reviewing and tweaking it to help is altogether different from bashing through another person's responsibilities without consent.

Tip #78: "Avoid Going Over Their Head"

When a coworker is not doing what we need and this is interfering with our job, going to their manager is a poor next move. The exception is if we share the same one. After all, we are supposed to tell ours of any troubles we run into, though it's still best to do it in person and with a smile. Afterward, send your manager a quick reminder email devoid of finger pointing. The goal of the email is posterity, that we told them on a certain date, if questioned. Do it under the guise of a friendly reminder because we know they're busy, and be aware it can be forwarded to the person we are squealing on, so be careful. It's our manager's job, not ours, to tell the other person's manager to get their guy moving on it.

Tip #79: "It's Not My Job Syndrome"

We all have job duties, and when a manager asks us to do something that isn't our job, it's tempting to point this out, but don't. This says quite loudly, "I'm not a team player." That our manager has asked us automatically makes it our job, even if it might be demeaning or even inappropriate. The best bet there might be to do a bad job of it so that they think twice about asking us again, but do not overdo it. Revenge in the corporate world is best had in petty ways that provide plausible deniability.

Tip #80: "Never Show Attitude"

People and work can be annoying, but it's seldom wise to reveal we've got an attitude about someone or something. The more warranted the annoyance is, the less it should be shown. The worse it is, the more we should feign amusement and good humor. This is a life skill to master. It can save our neck from the chopping block. If we want to bitch, that's what our friends and family are for!

CHAPTER THREE

It Ends

All good things must come to an end. Here we talk about the issues that arise when we are departing.

Threats to Your Job

Tip #81: "Lost Contracts Happen"

Our employer can lose a contract with a client and not have another to put us on. Now, instead of making them money by charging the client hourly for our services, we are costing our employer money, being on company overhead. Our days are numbered. Always start looking for a job when this happens, and even before, if we know a contract is ending on a certain date and there has been no word of an extension or renewal. Or other contracts. Hoping for the best can cost us financially when we are caught flatfooted and out the door, no prospects in sight.

Tip #82: "Our Manager's Assessment"

The most consistent threat to our job is your manager's opinion of us. This can change quickly and sometimes without merit. There is a reason people suck up, the theory being that managers don't get rid of people they like or who make them feel and/or look good. People can throw us under the bus to them behind our back, which is just one way a manager's opinion can sour without our understanding or even being aware. Always be on the lookout for disapproval, or a change in the winds, as it may herald a change of job.

Tip #83: "Performance Reviews Are Stupid"

The dreaded performance review is touted by HR as an opportunity to gracefully accept criticism and grow as a person and vital staff member who can better meet the company's needs, while humbly improving oneself. Instead, it's often a chance for managers to unnecessarily sow resentment. Trivial things are blown out of proportion, and achievements are tagged as us just doing our job and not worth noting. This can happen because managers do not want to be seen as praising everyone, so they look for faults, offending us in the process. And if there are performance bonuses to be had, they can purposely avoid praising us to avoid the payout (because management wants this).

Tip #84: "Budget Cuts"

These usually happen at a client, especially local, state, and federal governments. But budget cuts can happen anywhere and usually mean that a number of positions must be eliminated. Ours could be one of them, regardless of how critical the work we are doing is, or how well we have been performing it. If you are on a contract, find out when it renews and try to assess the likelihood that the position is safe. Be ready to jump ship if you sense it's not essential and budget cuts are announced.

Tip #85: "Unacceptable Work Changes"

Sometimes our employer essentially kills our job. Technically we will still have one and at the same pay, etc., but we might be assigned duties that are so different from what we have been doing, and even assigned a physical location or team that is far away, that we basically have a new job. Seldom is this change great. It's often job-ending, as they will place us somewhere that they need us, not somewhere we need to be. Object and we are not a team player. It may be time to depart.

Looking for New Work

Tip #86: "Employers Do Fire Those Looking to Leave"

It happens. Our employer learns we're looking for another job and fires us. The reasons vary, from assuming we will be unproductive going forward to revenge. It behooves us to hide it well. Sometimes they will admit it, and they may add insulting things about us or our work as additional justifications. We are not supposed to burn a bridge behind us, but sometimes the employer does it for us.

Tip #87: "Be Careful with Job Boards"

Long ago, job boards would let us prevent our current employer from seeing that our resume was active, but this potentially job-saving feature vanished. Now all we can do is go anonymous, which hurts our search. But still use it. See the previous tip for why!

Tip #88: "Do Stealth Interviews"

If we work in a casual attire environment but have an interview at lunch time, and for which we need to wear a suit and tie, showing up at work this way tips off our coworkers. Leave a tie in the car. The jacket, too, and not hanging up where those who recognize the car will see it. We might even need to change in a fast food restaurant, giving ourselves more time to prepare. The subterfuge can save our current job until we are ready to leave on our terms.

Tip #89: "Don't Talk at Work"

One problem with recruiters calling is just that – they're calling. Even if we say we can't talk details now, astute peers, especially those who know or sense we hate our job, might realize who we are talking to, especially if we are repeatedly overheard saying such things. Screen unknown calls and return them when the conversation poses little risk.

Tip #90: "Written Offer, Then Notice"

Never give notice at a job until a written offer from the new employer has been received. During negotiations, when asked how soon you can start, the best answer is "two weeks from the day I receive a written offer letter." The only real protection this offers us is unemployment benefits. If we quit the current job, then don't get the written offer (i.e. proof) that we had one lined up for the new job, and then file for unemployment, we are likely to be denied and get nothing to hold us over until another job. The appearance can also hurt us in our job search.

Impending Departures

Tip #91: "Two Weeks' Notice Can Get Us Fired"

Once we resign, employers sometimes fire us immediately instead of letting us complete the two weeks' notice we gave. This is more likely if there is tension at our job and our manager genuinely dislikes us. And if the joy of sticking it to us outweighs getting a smooth hand over of our work from us to someone else. If our project is dead and we are costing the company money instead of earning it for them, this can contribute to the decision. Why should they lose money over the next two weeks when they can make us be the one to take the loss?

Tip #92: "Ask the New Employer If You Can Start Early"

Due to the previous tip, we should always tell a new company if we need to give two weeks' notice. Then casually ask if we can start earlier on the off chance that our employer lets you go immediately when we give notice. The answer is typically yes. HR understands that this does indeed happen. Always ask as if you are certain it won't happen (implying everything is fine at your current job), not like it's expected (because things are not fine and maybe you are trouble that they should rethink about hiring).

Tip #93: "Two Weeks' Notice is Voluntary"

While it is good practice, no one can make us give two weeks' notice. Many U.S. states are "at will" employment, which means either party can terminate without warning. If our job is hostile, we likely don't want to go back, nor would they want us back, and they may show us the door the moment we give notice, when we are expecting two more weeks of work and pay. It can therefore be advantageous to give little notice. It will burn bridges, but they may already be burned. Use wisely, rarely, and cautiously.

Tip #94: "Give Notice at COB"

Always give notice after 3pm, or when less than an hour of the workday (or that of our boss) remains. It can cause anxiety to wait for a response all day if we gave notice via email. A reply will likely be there in the morning when we arrive, but at least we were gone and living our life, with this off our mind (mostly). Another option: giving notice is often better done in person (it is smoother and there's no waiting for a reaction), then followed up in writing for the record.

Tip #95: "Put a Good Spin on Being Fired"

If it happens, we need to make being fired sound as good as possible. We can admit to a mistake if we explain it well and seem like we learned something (and that it was innocent), but sometimes the firing is bullshit and we need more creativity. Companies will ask if they can contact former employers and we can decline in this case without even needing to explain that they're unlikely to say anything helpful because that's kind of obvious. This means a creative answer can pass the smell test if done well, precisely because no sniffing around is happening.

Before Leaving

Tip #96: "Grab Files"

Technically, anything we did at work belongs to our employer and we're not allowed to keep a copy, but they usually can't stop us. Files can be loaded on a pen drive or uploaded to sites like Dropbox. At the least, we might want work-related bookmarks from a browser, not to company sites, but online resources we consult. The reason for grabbing files is not to reinvent the wheel at other jobs. Whether it's code or documentation, we might regret not being able to leverage previous achievements, and having to start over. Employers offended by this should remember that staff may have brought files and knowledge from previous jobs when starting, and that they benefited from staff not starting from scratch.

Tip #97: "Visit Favorite Nearby Locations"

Saying goodbye is hard, even to great restaurants and dive bars near this job. We might visit them again, but maybe not. Visit one last time and get your favorite items, and bring a work friend if that's what you usually do. It may be your last outing together. They may even get the check.

Tip #98: "Network"

If we haven't already, right before leaving a job is a good time to get email addresses, phone numbers, and connect with people on LinkedIn. For the first two, strive for personal info because work ones do us no good when they leave the company, too. That's why LinkedIn is the best choice. We don't even have to ask, so much as find them there and connect.

Tip #99: "Reconnect with Past Team Members"

Sometimes we change teams at work and it can be good to make the rounds and catch up with people, especially before they know that we are leaving. Catching up is almost always appreciated, partly because everyone loves a good excuse to stop working for a minute. There is no real downside to doing this and it can also remind us why you liked working there, if we ever did, before we became unhappy enough to leave. Leaving on good terms is always good.

Tip #100: "Bury the Hatchet"

If there's tension between us and someone else, we may want to smooth it over before we are gone and it's too late. This can be as simple as being friendly rather than addressing the source of tension. Don't be surprised if an overture is met with surprise, indifference, or a brush off. At the least, we tried and get to own the high road. We can always ignore the subject, person, and tension, which is the easy way out, so taking a chance when we are leaving anyway gives an opportunity to grow as a person with little risk if it doesn't pan out.

On the Way Out

Tip #101: "Exit Interviews Can Only Hurt Us"

Do not say anything negative in an exit interview. The reason is that we are leaving and any problems at this job won't be ours once we walk out the door, so we literally have nothing to gain. Move on. We may want to return one day and a bitter exit interview can come back to haunt us. Even if we really want revenge on some staff, venting is unlikely to achieve anything.

Tip #102: "People Get Weird"

Once our departure is known, some people get weird about it. For example, they might no longer speak to us anymore than necessary. It's as if we have personally betrayed them. We might stop getting invited to casual group lunches or the morning coffee routine. If we were in a clique, we may be instantly out. It's as if we died and our ghost is haunting them and they'd just like us to go already. The day we give notice is the day our job ends in many ways, even if we will still be there for 10 more, painfully long working days. Don't take it personally.

Tip #103: "Leave Good Notes"

A good handover of our work to your manager, replacement, or team members is a great way to leave a strong, positive final impression. It's a way to remind them of what they're missing as we go. These will often be reviewed before we leave, but we can still omit something without them realizing it because we did (italics) give them a lot and they might be none the wiser. This can be a good compromise if we really hate them and want nothing to do with the request to do a handover.

Tip #104: "Ask for References Now"

Sometimes people will offer to be a reference, but most of the time, we will need to ask. We should already have a sense of who is going to say yes. Unless we have no other choice, there's little sense in asking a reluctant person, who might agree but then never return a reference check call. Or who will have less than stellar things to say. Choose wisely. All of this can be a reason to exit a job before it goes bad.

Tip #105: "Be Prepared to Take Your Stuff"

This might seem obvious, but some people do actually forget to take personal belongings, or some of them, when exiting, or they make it hard on themselves by not having a small box to do it in one trip. It is often good to do this before the last day, making a final exit easy because we are not carrying around a box while shaking hands one last time. Make the exit a baggage-free departure. It's both symbolic and practical.

After Leaving

Tip #106: "Goodbye is Forever"

We will probably never see these people again. The bigger the metropolis or industry we work in, the truer this is. We can follow each other on LinkedIn or exchange emails and phone numbers, but we have moved on and so have they. Few care about staying in touch in any meaningful way unless we became friends who did things outside of work together before one of us exits the job.

Tip #107: "Employers Lie to Unemployment Offices"

An employer is not above telling the state unemployment office that we were fired for conduct when this is a lie. If it's the company's fault that we are out of work, the state unemployment premiums that they must pay may rise, just like being at fault in a car accident, so they can save money – and cost us a lot – with this stunt. Our state may investigate, demanding proof from the employer that we were warned in writing about our supposed misconduct before being terminated. Without this proof, they are likely to rule in our favor.

Tip #108: "Don't Visit"

After our last day, it's considered weird to drop by for any reason other than official business, such as picking up or returning an item through HR. We can be looked at as an unwelcome interloper, a ghost from the past, or even a threat if we left on unfavorable terms. When we walk out that door on our last day, we should never return unless invited. Even then, expect a shocked, almost disgusted, suspicious look and, "What are *you* doing here?"

Tip #109: "Rate Them"

There are sites where we can leave a review about our experience at a company. Try to be as generic as possible so that the company cannot tell it's you. It's also wise to wait six months, especially if we have anything negative to say. They can't publicly identify you even if they figure out who wrote the review, but avoid giving HR an axe to grind about you if there's any chance a potential employer will be contacting them.

Tip #110: "Lose the Baggage"

A bad experience can give us an attitude that we carry forward into a new position like a poison we may not realize is in our system. Try to reflect on what went wrong, learn from experiences, and most importantly, don't let any problems cloud your attitude, outlook, and work performance going forward. This is giving bad actors too much influence over our present and future. Leave them behind in every way, not just as someone we don't interact with anymore, but as someone who doesn't continue to be an adverse influence on our happiness, fulfillment, and prospects.

These tips are drawn from *The Corporate Life Survival Guide*, which you can get at https://amzn.to/2RwRzBi or use the QR code below:

About the Author

Randy Zinn has worked as a software developer/architect and manager in the Washington D.C. area for over 20 years as an employee, contractor, or consultant through his own company. He's a proud father to a son (b. 2012) and daughter (b. 2016) and loves spending time with them when not playing golf, lap swimming, making music, or writing fiction. Under another name, he's published non-fiction and fantasy stories and released several albums of his music (hard rock and acoustic guitar). He holds a Bachelor of Music in classical guitar, Magna cum Laude.

He's also faced a variety of personal issues including Attention Deficit Disorder, speech problems, depression, suicide, bullying, being Learning Disabled, and a crippling tendonitis injury, all of which he overcame.

Connect with him online

http://www.Randy-Zinn.com
https://www.facebook.com/pg/randyzinnauthor

If you like this book, please help others enjoy it.

Lend it. Please share this book with others.
Recommend it. Please recommend it to friends, family, reader groups, and discussion boards
Review it. Please review the book at Goodreads and the vendor where you bought it.

JOIN THE RANDY ZINN NEWSLETTER!

Subscribers receive discounts, bonus content, and the latest promotions and updates. You also get a free digital copy of *Adventures in Opposite Land (The Memoir Shorts 1)*.

http://www.randy-zinn.com/newsletter

Randy Zinn Books

MEMOIRS
A Storm of Lies
Corporate Hell: A Memoir
Consulting Hell: A Memoir

A Silence Not So Golden Trilogy
Book 1: *Refusal to Engage: My Voice is Become Death*
Book 2: *A Blast of Light: My Rebirth Through Music*
Book 3: *The Wine-Dark Sea: My New Life Awaits*

The Memoir Shorts
Book 1: *Adventures in Opposite Land*
Book 2: *Am I Evil?*

OTHER NON-FICTION
The Corporate Life Survival Guide
Tips on Surviving Corporate Hell

View all books at Amazon:

www.ingramcontent.com/pod-product-compliance
Lightning Source LLC
Chambersburg PA
CBHW031036040426
42333CB00038BA/381